Feelings Poems

D0267437

Compiled by John Foster

Contents

Twenty-five metres   *Celia Warren*   2
Night fright   *Marian Swinger*   4
Mixed feelings   *Julie Holder*   6
Why did you pull her hair?   *John Foster*   8
Left out   *Celia Warren*   10
Bertie the hamster   *John Coldwell*   12
My new brother   *Eric Finney*
   and John Foster   14
Birthday surprises   *John Foster*   16

Acknowledgements

The Editor and Publisher wish to thank the following who have kindly given permission for the use of copyright material:

John Coldwell for 'Bertie the hamster' © 1995 John Coldwell; Eric Finney and John Foster for 'My new brother' © 1995 Eric Finney and John Foster; John Foster for 'Birthday surprises' and 'Why did you pull her hair?' both © 1995 John Foster; Julie Holder for 'Mixed feelings' © 1995 Julie Holder; Marian Swinger for 'Night fright' © 1995 Marian Swinger; Celia Warren for 'Left out' and 'Twenty-five metres' both © 1995 Celia Warren.

Twenty-five metres

Sam and I swam twenty-five metres.
Dad swam too. He wanted to beat us.
Sam swam like a fish.
I swam like a frog.
Dad swam like a dolphin
but he couldn't beat us
when Sam and I
swam twenty-five metres.

Then Dad said, 'I'm proud of you;
proud of your strength;
that's the very first time
that you both swam a length.'
Then he gave us a badge
and an ice-cream to treat us.
I am proud of my badge;
it says '25 Metres'.

Celia Warren

Night fright

My hair stood on end
and I trembled with fright
when I heard a strange noise
on the stairs in the night.

'CREAK', it went.
'EEK', I went.
What should I do?
Then my brother
leaped into my room
and yelled, 'BOO!'

Marian Swinger

Mixed feelings

I stayed at my friend's
And that made me glad.
I wanted to play
With a toy that she had;
She said that I couldn't
And that made me mad.

I shouted at her
That made me feel bad.
And now we're not friends
And that makes me feel sad.

Julie Holder

Why did you pull her hair?

I told my friend a secret.
She promised not to tell.
My friend told her friend.
She told her friend as well.

Now, everyone knows my secret.
I think that it's unfair.
I told my friend I trusted her.
That's why I pulled her hair.

John Foster

Left out

It feels as if pins
Are pricking my eyes.
My face is burning hot.
A firework is trying
To go off inside me.
My feet are glued to the spot.
My hands are rocks in my pockets.
I want to run away.
But my legs are rooted to the ground
Like trees. I have to stay
And listen
To everyone calling me names
And not letting me
Join in with their games.

Celia Warren

Bertie the hamster

Every Sunday I clean Bertie's cage.
I tip his bedding into the bin,
I give his food to the birds,
I pour his water down the sink.

But today there is no Bertie to put back.
Dad says that he had a good life
and two is very old for a hamster.
I look into his empty cage
And remember his soft nose,
His warm fur,
And his tiny body sitting on my hand.

John Coldwell

My new brother

We used to be three—
Mum, Dad and me.
But now there's another.
My new baby brother.

He cries in the night
And sleeps in the day.
He hasn't any idea
Of how to play.

My baby brother's name is Joe.
I just can't wait for him to grow.

Eric Finney and John Foster

Birthday surprises

When I see my presents
on my birthday
I feel excited.
I wonder what surprises are
hiding inside.

When I open my presents
on my birthday
I feel delighted
as I see the surprises
hiding inside.

John Foster